THE INVENTION OF ZERO

THE
INVENTION
OF ZERO
An Accumulation of Poems by
MIKE AQUILINA

PITTSBURGH:
Serif Press
2020

For Terri

Table of Contents

The Invention of Zero

In ages past I could not have expressed
numerically your difference from the rest
of everything encountered here below,
of everything that's made *ex nihilo.*

From Antioch and Rome there came no sign
to mark the place beside the number line.
A city could produce an epic hero,
but not a jot to represent a zero.

In India the mathematicians found
the notion that we render in the round.
They registered as first to hold the thought
of what should stand when all has come to naught.

From nothing all is made; and nothing lasts.
It's striking, now, how everything contrasts
with you, as if the world were binary
and you the only 1, at least for me.

（2）

A Trick of Light

It is the only memory I've kept
of Disneyland: the specters as they swept
in luminescent pairs across the floor.
They were just light and shadow, nothing more.

Yet they were tall as Mom and thick as Dad.
Their form fit the dimensions they had had
in life, presumably, before they came
to Disney's haunted mansion and to fame.

What could I do, at six, with such a sight?
Could dancing couples be a trick of light?
Surveying every shade as it went by,
I swear a pretty lady caught my eye.

And now I am much older and I find
I too am a projection of a kind,
a hologram held up by superstrings.
(A physicist can clarify such things.)

Is anything substantial as it looks?
Now pages are not paper in my books.
Still, watching all the shades as they go by,
I swear a pretty lady caught my eye.

（4）

Jordan

"For this reason the Savior was baptized
to sanctify all the waters."
— Clement of Alexandria

Did it surge — and did it overtake the banks —
did placid water ripple back to source —
did jubilation call a change of course —
did river stones rise up to give him thanks?

The Fathers say the waters that we know
were once, like every element, accursed,
till John beheld his kinsman and immersed
him wholly in the transhistoric flow.

They say now every drop must bear the grace
by way of mist and cloud to find the font
and cycle ages to supply the want
of living water from that distant place.

The sea cannot but roar and bank its waves.
The flood must clap its hands because it saves.

(6)

S.CALLISTUS.M

Callistus

Tertullian tore his dalmatic.
Hippolytus had a cow.
Both became schismatic
when Callistus stood the prow.

He had a heart for sinners,
for concubines and such.
His patience with beginners
they found a bit too much.

They fled from the forgiving,
the laxity and taints.
But there's hope for all us living
if all three died as saints.

The Deal

Is Solitaire itself if you're nearby,
or must it simply cease to hold the name?
Does it count, without a chill, without a sigh?
If not a metaphor, is it the same?

Or should we even say that it's a game?
I win when all my options have run dry!
I could not wish to issue any blame
if fate should stop me just a seven shy.

They tell me there's no balm a man can buy
for loneliness, no recompense to claim.
The cards hold out no hope of victory.
A loss is but a shrug and not a shame.

Yet fate itself is toothless and is tame
when we sit together, you and I.
I dealt a solitude, but then you came.
To call it what it was would be a lie.

Because Science

Here, it seems, the rules begin to wither.
The flow can go to yon and still come hither.
A bit can bilocate and then behave
as if it were instead some kind of wave.

What Planck took for a trick turned up a fact
as Einstein wrote the drama's second act.
The universe is much as we had feared.
The smaller something gets the more it's weird.

I'm told that such ideas have consigned
Aquinas to the dustbin of the mind
and rendered Aristotle obsolete
for positing a ground beneath our feet.

And who am I to make the judgment call?
When sizing up the girls I chose the small.
Then suddenly the ground began to fly
and particles to wave as they went by.

Can it be good for atoms so to split?
"Tantum quantum," says the Jesuit.

Your Story, Morning Glory

My daughter Grace speaks to Mary Lou Williams.

Dancing's what you do across those keys —
but not the moves I measured in ballet.
It's like the sudden solo ecstasies
I dance on every family wedding day.

You vanish into melody and time.
You syncopate but never sink the tune.
You render the anticipated rhyme
as somehow on the dot a beat too soon.

I want to dance the way you build a chord
from scraps of sharp and natural and flat,
choosing not as men but as the Lord,
surprising as a syllable in scat.

Palimpsest

Erasure was their art, those cowled men.
Unbinding books, they blanched away the lines
with lye to clear the space a fresher pen
could fill with newer uncial designs.

That every obsolescence might be stripped,
they took a slender blade, as if to silk,
across the balky blots of ancient script
and left a page as pure as honeyed milk.

And yet beneath the new remained the haunt
of Tacitus, or Cicero perhaps,
waiting for the hour the world might want
to summon him from overlying maps.

But I say there is no art that can efface
your name or write another in its place.

The Future of Flesh

For Terri

While aging down to elemental glue —
the fated end of every horse's ass —
I pray to say more plainly what is true
before what comes for all must come to pass.

I've read that dinosaurs were once this way,
as tottering and lumbering as I.
They decomposed to carbon and one day
awoke as diamonds, clear as summer sky.

And now they shine and cannot be destroyed,
temples of the sun they seized in youth;
and, hard against the summons of the void,
they speak of beauty's all-enduring truth.

Sweet Nature! May I wake to clarity,
alight with her, whatever I shall be.

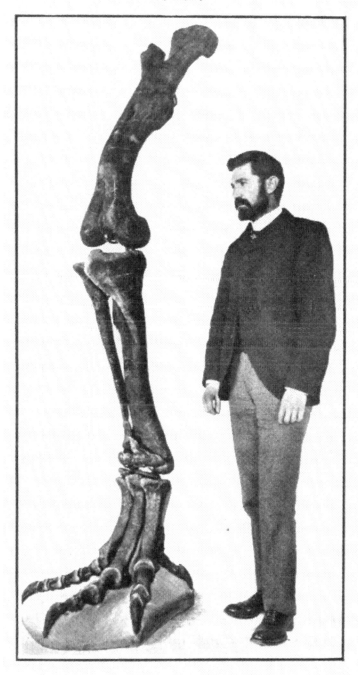

HERSCHEL'S FORTY-FOOT REFLECTING TELESCOPE.

FRB
Or, Love's Inconstancy

"Scientists have discovered the first Fast Radio Burst that beats at a steady rhythm, and the mysterious repeating signal is coming from the outskirts of another galaxy."

What are you saying, neutron star,
half a billion light years far?
And why should I be so accursed,
to hear you in a four-day burst —
and then for twelve days not a sound?

It's clear your signal is for me.
There is no other I can see
to audit you, not near or distant
or even possibly existent.
No other finder has been found

in spite of centuries of searches
in planetaria and churches.
As object of your inattention,
I'm obligated here to mention
this pattern that I've come to know.

You loved me all those years ago?

The Father of the Dancer

For Grace

A man who makes his living at a desk
is ill-prepared to step up to the barre.
He finds his proper place inside the car
that bears the girl who bends in arabesque.

Some men, it seems, should rather keep their pants
than trade them for a spangled leotard.
To lift a leg's the same as falling hard,
and so must end their first and final dance.

Such a man can understand ballet
as pageantry of things he cannot do
with muscles that, alas, he never grew
now raised up high with every relevé.

I cannot find the plot or even trace
intention in the choreography.
Nonetheless, I'll say this much for me:
I know it when I see it — and it's Grace.

The Open Boat

In the way of dreams I didn't know why
we were rowing against a storm that day.
Our craft, like every wave, was gray,
and none of us knew the color of the sky.

Nor did I know my mates at oar.
I never even saw their eyes.
We dared not turn. We could not rise.
I had not ever rowed before.

Yet I knew that this I had to do:
pull through the floods that roiled the bay
and swamped the bridge along the way,
the way that stretched from me to you.

(23)

Aquilina Men

Fac et spera, the family motto,
makes more trouble than it ought to.
It is, alas, a sorry fact
that we are more inclined to act
first and then much later cope
by the ardor of our hope.
I *make* these hasty lines for you.
I *hope* that they, in turn, will *do*.
You recognize, I'm sure, the cycle
handed down from Mike to Michael.

Kidney Stone

I wake up of a sudden in a rage —
a rage of pain I've learned I can withstand.
I am a child, no matter what my age,
and quieted if I but reach my hand

to touch your sleeping form. Then I can see
why death may do its worst yet have no sting.
No distance keeps my paradise from me —
no distance from the shadow to the thing.

The heavenly Jerusalem will come
one day and take away our pain and tears.
Yet even now I see the city from
the pillow where I've laid my head for years.

What poet ever did this:
rolled up tubes of city crowds,
hurled sheets of steel into the clouds,
and watched them sailing skyward?
His name would be a byword,
his reputation never shorten
in anthologies of Norton,
his lines the student ever glean
for seeds of what they maybe mean.
Your love has made me so insane
I wish that I could build a plane.

IUVAT EVASISSE
Virg:3. æn.

Incunabulum

Every blessed page they press
from a single sculpted wooden block,
which can just one tale confess
and then return to closet stock.

Each letter shaved into relief
awaits anew the bath of black.
The binder cuts the final sheaf
and shakes a calfskin from the rack.

The incunabulum, it seems,
is suited best to sacred things,
to missals and to mystic dreams,
to saints and testaments of kings.

I'd have your story told this way,
with a block apart for just your name
pressed in red as if to say
that *this* in all the world is flame —

that this in all the world is worth
the labors of these artisans —
that this in all the orb of earth
deserves the parchment, ink, and skins.

An incunabulum might do
for publishing the word abroad
of the love I have for you
and other prodigies of God.

Incandescent

It was Edison killed the sunset

with electricity
that raced through bulbs and coils
and did what lamps and oils
could never do for me.

It was Edison snuffed the sunrise

and made it obsolete
by assembling the alarms
to rouse our family farms
to bottled light and heat.

But Edison made no plan for you,

who rendered him undone.
It's you who make the nights grow dark,
you who make the day embark,
my rising, setting sun.

Before Sleep

As the hillside holds the snow,
as the summit holds the glow
of the sunset, even so.

Sonnet in Spray Paint

The cosmos is an urban overpass
  or maybe a bodega's outer wall,
created out of nothing to amass
effusions from a can of aerosol.
I am that can, an angel sent to tag
and tease a sense of substance from a glyph
curvaceous in your praise. I do not brag;
I'm not the one to draw an is from if.
But only insofar as I suggest
what I behold in heaven I succeed.
The limits of the cosmos are the test.
Such limits, I suppose, are what I need.
    By night I spray but what an angel must,
    though every hasty scrawl will be unjust.

Hardball
For Thom Tracy

Two white
 infinities
stretched tight
and stitched in red:
a world of fearful
symmetries.
Jehovah's might:
my brother Ned.

Ned towers,
across the grass.
He powers
the planet's arc,
measured, careful
not to pass
the boy who cowers
at the edge of the park.

To a child so small,
Ned is all.
"Tommy, keep your eye on the ball."

At the Corner of Business & Memory

You are city traffic in my day;
my mind, you know, a one-way street.
At nine o'clock you're fifteen feet
through intersections, blocking way
for what I was about to say.

This boardroom needs a traffic cop
to press you on — "Let's move it, doll" —
to blow his whistle, waving all
my thoughts of business to the top
of midday hills. Again they stop

for flashing lights and tracks and trains
of thought. A siren blares and wanes.
Then, speeding cross the passing lanes
come you! You wink at work, and then
it's back, sweet gridlock, once again.

Toward a Metaphysics of My Son

Even for your age you're small.
I wonder where you fit it all:
substance, essence, person, form.
I wonder how you keep it warm.

You toddle wobbling all your *ens*.
From here I smell your accidents.
You call no category home.
You're in the *esse*, not the poem.

Simeony

I thought it was the melody,
the Red Book *Nunc Dimittis* she
would hum above her needlepoint.
Is it tones in sequence that anoint —
can modals transubstantiate —
a man come to his senses late,
n thing that passes for his heart?
I bought the hymnal, then, to chart
and so possess, and so contain
the seeming sacramental strain
that healed and held when merely heard
in peace according to her word.

Yet more than word — it is her voice
that changes me. It is the choice
of heaven and her rite to bless
one man with chanted tenderness.

River Music

Somewhere in the Pennsylvania wild,
two rivers meet to form a third: A child
arrives to upset their bed, divert their streams,
transpose their river songs and river dreams.

Oh, they'll sing and dream them still, but now in G,
the key of glaciers gone and gravity.
So children change one's beds, and banks, and warp.
But the key of G will always keep one sharp.

The Sound at the Back of the Office

Snap. The trap captures
something—maybe a mouse,
perhaps it's just a poem.

What god is it that raptures
such creatures to my house
as to a heaven home?

For one the god's a crevice,
some flaw of brick or mortar,
beside a warming flue.

But a poem sees a promise
of a rather different order,
strives upwardly to you.

Terms and Conditions

If you take out any term, the others vanish.
Our T&Cs are freedom, love, and hell.
This is, I think, the thought we'd like to banish.

It's true in Portuguese and even Spanish.
It's true in any place you choose to dwell.
If you take out any term, the others vanish.

Drop hell. The world goes beige or maybe tannish.
Love dies unless it makes you feel unwell.
This is, I think, a thought we'd like to banish.

Forsaking love, the boy becomes more mannish,
they say; it's after Eve that Adam fell.
But take out any term, the others vanish.

When trendy authors go dystopianish
and liberty no longer rings their bell,
they type the kind of thoughts we'd rather banish.

We're restless and we'd really rather plan a sh-
uffling of the terms that cast our spell.
But if you take out any term, the others vanish.
This is, I think, the thought we'd like to banish.

Litany of the Fathers

St. Epiphanius: Bring me the balm from your Medicine Chest.

St. Augustine: Show me the place where a heart can find rest.

St. Athanasius: May I always awake on the right side of truth.

St. Ignatius: Even in age may I love like a youth.

St. Justin: Teach me to search out the seeds of the Word.

St. Polycarp: May my soul fly the sky, at the end, like a bird.

St. Melito: Give me love for the past that prepared for the Christ.

St. Jerome: Let me growl, now and then, with a touch of the feist.

St. Clement: May my heart find the poem in every thing.

St. Ephrem: May I always know just when to shut up and sing.

(*54*)

Terri

I'll sing your antecedents to your descendants.
Your roots are the mysterium tremendens.
It took us three millennia to assemble
our *terr-* from Greek *tremein,* which is "to tremble."

What frightens any Latins is terrific.
The concept can't be put in hieroglyphic.
If we try to make our fears a bit more bearable,
we still must render them as something terrible.

They tried to make you harmless as a froth
by naming fuzzy towels terrycloth.
In spite of all these efforts, you loom scarier.
I know that you could not be any terrier.

The Apocalyptic Rag

It's so elegant
So intelligent
— *T.S. Eliot*

When Rome eternal falls,
when Vandals breach the walls,
I'll take the trouble
to crawl through the rubble
to you, to you.

If a sliver of roof remains
to shelter us from the rains,
I'll raise no alarms,
I'll open my arms
to you, to you.

When the forum has fallen to ruin,
and we can't buy a pot to catch dew in,
I'll have all I need
for me and my breed
in you, in you.

When the music has all been wrung
from the words of our native tongue,
I'll write you in Runic:
"You won't need that tunic,
just you, just you."

All rage and all worry I shed
in the place where we make our bed.
Here history tends.
    Say goodbye to the *gens*.
        This my mind comprehends:
            All's well when it ends
        with you.

Why Do the Swine Get All the Pearls?

For a Country Singer from the Bronx

I drive below the limit down the avenue,
and all the girls I dream about come into view,
and each one has a guy who's messing with her curls.
Why do the swine get all the pearls?

I pay for one admission to the pleasure park.
The couples ride the coasters as the sky goes dark.
I see them on the ferris wheels and tilt-a-whirls.
Why do the swine get all the pearls?

I never know the lines that I'm supposed to say.
I search my sorry soul from now to yesterday.
And I'm sitting in my Chevy while the hot rods win the
  girls.
Why do the swine get all the pearls?

I'll buy a ship and sail it cross the northern sea.
I'll be a billionaire and dine with royalty.
And I'll put the same sad question to the kings and
  dukes and earls.
Why do the swine get all the pearls?

Indulgence

Lent! I curse the meat, the nicotine,
take the holy stairs with grudging knees.
Fridays, trudge the stations while sixteen
pounds of baby sleeps and drools and pees
upon my shoulder.
I stand a colder
room. Forego the thermostat.
And still not penitential for all that,
I search my heart for reasons, finding these:
Your hair is long, lush, and brown, blown clean
across my pillow when I wake. Each breeze
brings the songs you sing our son.
                    My queen!
As king, I wrongly spend this holy Lent.
Though I give up all but you, I shall not want.

The Chill of Distance

Is there a working furnace in this place?
Or is it just I'm far from you
that makes my lips and fingers blue
and slows my heart and grims my face?

I'm unaccustomed to the draft
that comes to fill the space beside
the place where I am occupied.
Can I be warm where you've not laughed?

Or can my lifeblood make its way
if air itself observes a law
that lets me not begin to thaw
till you appear and smile and stay.

Telecommunications

Some hundred miles of cable span the skies
and stretch beneath the streets from you to me.
Expensive men and instruments assize
your signal strength and tone and clarity.

But where's the gauge to count or man to mark
the elements conveyed across the wire
each time you call: the copper takes the spark
and bears your voice, your warmth, your light, your
    fire.

To My Wife and Son

If I had a piano, I'd write you songs, I would,
and I'd hurl the kitchen table away,
roll the upright monster in,
pull you two from your nursery — and play.
Then you'd dance a wild merengue there,
from windowed wall to windowed wall.
The neighbors and their dog, of course,
would watch you swing my son about.
And as children at the bus stop gasped,
lighted cigarettes would fall
like comets by the dozen
from a dozen boundless teenage skies.

And I would hurl each ostinato to
your reeling, loving, pounding heart.
My son would catch each desperate
glissando in his Latin soul.
And just as all of Canonsburg
had gathered and the cops arrived,
I'd make my banging hands reveal
my bassest motivations:
I'd throw a thousand low and Latin
chords to each and every wall.
And then I'd stand and turn and with
the town I'd watch you drop,
exhausted, laughing, holding
tightly one another...

It's all a lie, of course, you know.
I have two left hands and two left ears.
And every piano's out of tune.

But believe me, I would.

1

1

1

1

To Be, or Not

I toil and spin to seem to have a heart
half-worth your love. To seem is twice the art.
I fly from final chance to final chance.
A cinder in the wind would seem to dance,
but shatters should the wind hold back a breath.
For you to leave me, Love, would be my death.

Epithalamium

Let us feast tonight with Cana's guest
and beg his blessing on your vow.
Lord Jesus bids you come to taste
the good wine you have kept till now.

Mis Senoras de la Leche

Cradled at your breast,
in God's good image made,
my child, my little Christ,
twirls the fairest mother's braid.

Night Watch

For this is the good: To look upon one who looks back.
— *Augustine*

A bay by night relays the stars, returns the dim
glow of a waning crescent moon.
So dark, your eyes reflect the light of infant eyes
that close to love as sleep comes soon.
You look and love looks back to you, from deep to deep.
A constellation in your gaze
glows goodnight. A sky and sea in green and blue
ripple tide to close our days.

The Sphinx

How do you answer the riddle?
The Sphinx is at the door and wants to know.

This poem, I said, can have no middle
or end. Please tell the Sphinx to go.

You could not stop the winter storm for me

You could not stop the winter storm for me.
So you built a house and kept it warm for me.

You could not stop the world's alarms for me.
Instead you opened up your arms for me.

You could not keep my childhood here for me.
So you gave me children, drew them near for me.

Could heaven be more close than this for me?
God made your healing, saving kiss for me.

More, more my world is here

More, more my world is here.
I wake, I work, I stay
where I can know you near.

Your curtains keep my day.
Your bed describes my night.
We sleep while angels pray

that I may never stray,
not far nor long from sight
of Love, by day, by night.

The Poem of the Act of the Mind

Nearness is a thing the mind decrees
belying all statistics and the facts.
It scans the far horizons, and it sees
two scattered stars and instantly contracts
a billion miles to make a lion's mane.
A mind can make of distant lights a fish.
It's hardly sensible or even sane
to think that stars come true upon a wish.

Yet there we were: as disparate as stars
that serve to mark the range from bright to dim.
Who could conjure up a train from bumper cars?
What Mind immortal and what eye could skim
creation and descry and so decree
a constellation ranged from you to me?

Pilgrimage

Some years are Rome.
You arrive at them, and you are home.
They're furnished with a loving touch.
They feed you right. They feed you much.

Others are the Holy Land,
a place of unrelenting sand,
except for now and then a rock,
yet still a place where God can walk.

One alone will be a ruin,
a Petra, an abandoned dune.
Unfinished, it will make the case
that here we have no lasting place.

My hope is this, this hope is true:
that I get there before you do.
You are my map, you make a way
I could not know unless you stay.

Man

To find the perfect wife he often looks —
or tastes — among the crockery of cooks.

He'll search among the crannies and the nooks
for the woman into whom he'll set his hooks.

A naturist will seek her by the brooks,
a chess aficionado mid the rooks.

A synod's worth of bishops with their crooks
can't pull me from the one I found in books.

Reality TV

"Children, be on your guard against idols."
— 1 John 5:21

You watch in fascination the Extremes —
the families consumed by single quirks.
The unreality of fever dreams
is metaphysic to their faith and works.

The Joneses cede their household to a hoard
and roll colossal balls of foil and twine,
their living room a chapel where adored
is rubbish that somehow became divine.

And down the street a couple never spends
a penny more than coupons on their fare.
Their heaven is a dumpster that forfends
all hunger for elect who worship there.

Then last the camera trains itself on me,
who watch you while you're watching a TV.

His Title His Glory

When his sister reached the end of earthly days,
Gregory the bishop preached her praise.
He eulogized her virtues in his verse
and homilized her spouse in terms no worse.

"He was her husband,"
  he noted by the way.
"I know of nothing more I need to say."

The Last M.A.

He'll know good poems when he dies.
That's what purgatory's for.
There a bright, angelic corps
wield swords of fire to excise
the scales from callow critics' eyes.

He'll know what's good, what works, what rhymes
objectively, not by his taste,
and roundabout his flabby waist
a hair shirt will atone for crimes
of a deconstructive life and times.

Then, one day, the Deity
will call forth all to meet the Muse
and hear from her the great Good News:
"This, oh, this is Poetry."
And at last even the Ph.D.
will step forth for his Master's degree.

Notes on the Poems

Because Science. Tantum quantum is Latin for *insofar as* or *inasmuch as*. St. Ignatius Loyola employed the phrase to explain the use of created goods. We use them "Insofar as they help us" to achieve the end for which we were created. We reject them "insofar as they hinder us."

Simeony. "Red Book" refers to the Lutheran *Service Book and Hymnal* in use in the mid-twentieth century. The Lutheran liturgy then concluded with an English translation of the *Nunc Dimittis* (Luke 2:29-32). Its chant setting was composed by Regina Holmen Fryxell.

Night Watch. The epigraph is from St. Augustine's Sermons 69.2.

His Title His Glory. St. Gregory of Nazianzus's Oration 8 is a eulogy for his sister Gorgonia. The quotation in the last couplet, about Gorgonia's husband Alypius, is a verbatim translation of Gregory's text.

Made in the USA
Columbia, SC
25 April 2023

15462716R00062